HORSES
AND
PONIES
FOREVER

Nicola Jane Swinney

Quarto is the authority on a wide range of topics.

Quarto educates, entertains and enriches the lives of our readers—enthusiasts and lovers of hands-on living.

www.quartoknows.com

Author: Nicola Jane Swinney
Editor: Harriet Stone
Designer: Melissa Alaverdy

First published in 2019 by QEB Publishing,
an imprint of The Quarto Group.
6 Orchard Road, Suite 100
Lake Forest, CA 92630
T: +1 949 380 7510
F: +1 949 380 7575
www.QuartoKnows.com

A CIP record for this book is available from the Library of Congress.

ISBN 978 0 7112 4642 3

Manufactured in Guangdong, China TT062019

9 8 7 6 5 4 3 2 1

MIX
Paper from responsible sources
FSC® C016973
www.fsc.org

The Forever Fabulous Stats contain information about the color, size, and "fabulous rating" of each breed.

Forever Fabulous Stats

Color	All colors
Size	12 to 13 hands high
🤍☁️	✓✓✓✓
★★★	Chincoteagues drink so much water that they can look fat!

A "hand" is a measurement 4 inches (10 cm) long. It is used to measure the height of a horse or pony.

Contents

Akhal-Teke

Akhal-Tekes originally lived in the desert.
They're the shiniest horses you will ever see!

Forever Fabulous Stats

Color	All solid colors
Size	16 hands high
♥♥♥	✓✓✓✓✓
★★★	The Queen of England's grooms tried to wash the shine off her Akhal-Teke!

In the sunlight, Akhal-Tekes shine like gold. The breed is very old. These horses came from the desert in Asia, so they are tough and don't need much food. They form a strong bond with their rider.

American Mustang

This is the United States' most famous horse.
It is one of the last wild breeds left in the world.

Forever Fabulous Stats

Color	All colors
Size	Up to 16 hands high
♥♥♥	✓✓✓✓
★★★	The name "Mustang" comes from the Spanish word, mesteno, which means "stray."

Mustangs are related to the first horses brought to America by the Spanish, in the 1500s. Some of those horses escaped to live in the wild. There were once around two million Mustangs roaming free across the United States.

American Quarter Horse

Small and sturdy, this breed can run like the wind!

Forever Fabulous Stats

Color	All colors
Size	Up to 15 hands high
🖤🖤	✓✓✓✓
⭐⭐	Quarter Horses got their name because they can run very fast for a quarter of a mile.

Around 700 years ago, owners would race American Quarter Horses along country lanes and across fields. They bet lots of money on these one-on-one races. Quarter Horses were also known for their "cow sense" which made them good at herding cattle.

Andalusian

Andalusians stand out in horse shows, because of their fiery beauty and flashy stride.

Forever Fabulous Stats

Color	Gray, black, bay, or chestnut
Size	Up to 16 hands high
♥♥♥	✓✓✓✓✓
★★★	The Andalusian is known as the noble aristocrat of the horse world.

Horses have lived in Spain and Portugal for thousands of years. These glorious horses were almost lost, because people used them in battles. They were saved by a group of monks. Today the breed is prized for its sporting ability and good looks.

Appaloosa

Striking spots make this lovely horse stand out from the crowd.

Forever Fabulous Stats

Color	Many colors
Size	From 14 hands high
♥♥	✓✓✓✓
★★★	The Appaloosa are named after the Palouse River in the U.S.

Spotted horses were prized by the Nez Perce Native Americans. The tribe bred the horses to get more and more spots! Appaloosas have seven different coat patterns. They also have striped hooves.

Arab

The Arab is one of the world's oldest breeds, and also perhaps the most beautiful.

Forever Fabulous Stats

Color	All solid colors, except palomino
Size	15 hands high
❤️❤️	✓✓✓✓✓
⭐⭐	The Arab horse has been used to improve other breeds.

With their tiny ears and "dished" (curved) faces, the Arab looks like something from a fairy tale. They have long manes and long tails which they hold up high. Thousands of years ago, Arab horses lived in tents with their owners. They still love people to this day.

Brumby

Brumbies are as much a part of Australia as Mustangs are of North America.

Forever Fabulous Stats

Color	All colors
Size	All sizes
♥♥	✓✓✓
★★★	Brumbies live in small groups in the wild, known as mobs or bands.

There were no horses in Australia until people arrived from Great Britain, in 1788. The boat journey from Britain was very long, so the horses that survived the trip were tough. Some escaped and bred in the wild in Australia. They were very clever and people were not able to catch them.

Camargue

These beautiful, ghostly white animals are known as "Horses of the Sea."

Forever Fabulous Stats

Color	Gray
Size	14 hands high
♥♥♥	✓✓✓✓
★★★	The Camargue is one of the oldest breeds in the world.

Camargue horses live in a triangle of marshland in France. The area is very hot in summer and icy cold in winter, so the animals are tough. They have lived there since prehistoric times.

Caspian

Caspians are good-looking and elegant animals. They are perfectly miniature.

Forever Fabulous Stats

Color	Bay, black, gray, or chestnut
Size	11 hands high
🖤🖤	✓✓✓✓
⭐⭐⭐	Although they are small, Caspians are horses, not ponies.

The Caspian breed was thought to be extinct for 1,000 years. Then a herd was found living near the Caspian Sea in Asia. Pretty little Caspians can be seen in ancient artwork that is 2,500 years old.

Chincoteague

Gentle, sturdy, and sweet-tempered, the Chincoteague makes an ideal pony to own.

Forever Fabulous Stats

Color	All colors
Size	12 to 13 hands high
♥♥♥	✓✓✓✓
★★★	Chincoteagues drink so much water that they can look fat!

These ponies live on the island of Assateague, off the east coast of America. They swim to the next island, Chincoteague, every year. The people who guide them across the water are known as "saltwater cowboys."

23

Clydesdale

The mighty Clydesdale is a gentle giant, with fluffy "feathered" feet.

Forever Fabulous Stats

Color	Bay, black, brown, or chestnut
Size	17 hands high or more
♥♥♥	✓✓✓✓✓
★★★	Clydesdales lift their feet as they walk, showing the bottom of each hoof.

There were once 140,000 horses in Scotland, and most of them were Clydesdales. These handsome animals were bred to be big. They were used for farm work and for pulling carts. Despite their size, they are calm and gentle.

Connemara

The Connemara is Ireland's only native breed. It is good-looking and athletic.

Forever Fabulous Stats

Color	All solid colors
Size	Up to 14 hands high
♥♥	✓✓✓✓✓
★★★	Connemaras are brave but kind.

Dun-colored (gray-gold or tan) ponies were brought to Ireland 2,500 years ago. They mated with the wild horses that lived on the western coast. Today, they make excellent sporting ponies.

27

Dales

The pretty Dales' muzzle (nose) is small enough to drink from a teacup!

Forever Fabulous Stats

Color	Black, brown, bay, gray, or roan (white plus another color)
Size	Up to 14 hands high
🖤🖤🖤	✓✓✓✓
⭐⭐⭐	Dales are strong but very gentle.

Dales ponies come from the north of England. They used to transport metal from the mines to the coast. They were very strong and very fast. Dales ponies are still famous for their wonderful trot, as well as their tough and obedient nature.

Dartmoor

Hardy and helpful, the charming little Dartmoor is always popular.

Forever Fabulous Stats

Color	Bay, brown, black, gray, chestnut, or roan
Size	12 hands high
❤️❤️🖤	✓✓✓✓✓
⭐⭐⭐	Dartmoors look like a small version of the middleweight hunter horse.

Wild ponies roamed the moors of southwest England for thousands of years. They were once used in Dartmoor prison to move prisoners around the grounds. Today they are well known as riding and show ponies.

Dutch Warmblood

Warmblood horses are calmer and quieter than hotblooded horses, like the Thoroughbred.

Forever Fabulous Stats

Color	Chestnut, bay, black, or gray
Size	Up to 17 hands high
🖤🖤	✓✓✓✓
⭐⭐	Dutch Warmbloods have won many medals in the Olympic Games.

Warmblood horses are popular for sporting events. The Dutch Warmblood is handsome, athletic, calm, and easy to train. It competes in dressage, showjumping, and three-day eventing.

Exmoor

These lovely ponies roam free across Exmoor in southwest England.

Forever Fabulous Stats

Color	Brown with a pale muzzle	
Size	Up to 12 hands high	
🖤☁️	✓✓✓✓✓	
⭐⭐	Ponies like the Exmoor have been around for 60,000 years.	

Not many horses are able to survive in harsher weather than Exmoor ponies. They have a double coat, a snow chute (thick tail hairs that funnel the snow), and hooded eyes, called "toad eyes," that protect them from the wind and rain.

Falabella

Small but perfectly formed, the Falabella is a little horse, not a pony.

Forever Fabulous Stats

Color	All colors
Size	Up to 5 hands high
🖤🖤	✓✓✓✓
⭐⭐⭐	The little Falabella will live happily in your house!

Horses came to the Americas in the 1500s. Some escaped and lived wild in the plains of Argentina. To survive the hot sun and El Pampero (the strong winds that blow across the plains), the Falabella became smaller and smaller. Today they are bred to stay tiny.

Fell

Fell ponies were once known as Galloways. They carried items across the Pennine Hills in England.

Forever Fabulous Stats

Color	Black, brown, gray, or bay (brown with a black tail)
Size	Up to 14 hands high
♥♥♥	✓✓✓✓
★★★	The name "Fell" comes from the old Viking word for hills.

Fell ponies are a close relative of the Dales. They have been known as a breed since the Roman times. Fells lived wild on the hills of northern England and were used to carry material and food across the land.

Florida Cracker

Small, neat, and smart, the Florida Cracker was a cowboys' favorite horse.

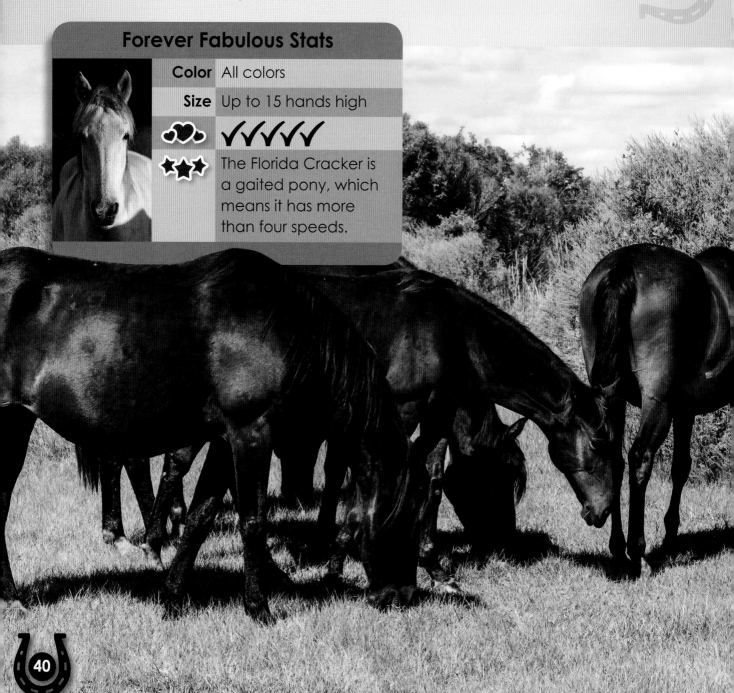

Forever Fabulous Stats

Color	All colors
Size	Up to 15 hands high
♥♥♥	✓✓✓✓✓
★★★	The Florida Cracker is a gaited pony, which means it has more than four speeds.

Florida cowboys were nicknamed "crackers" because of the sound made when they cracked their whips. Their little horses were known by the same name. They are very comfortable to ride with their flatfoot walk, running walk, and slow amble.

Friesian

These horses are real black beauties! They have a long mane, a long tail, and lots of spark.

Forever Fabulous Stats

Color	Black
Size	15 hands high
♥♥♥	✓✓✓✓✓
★★★	The Friesian is kind and loyal.

Friesians used to carry knights in armor. Now they make wonderful riding horses. They are easy to train, very good at sports, and look good pulling a carriage.

Hackney

The Hackney is said to be the "best carriage horse in the world."

Forever Fabulous Stats

Color	Bay, brown, black, or chestnut
Size	Up to 16 hands high
🖤🖤	✓✓✓✓
⭐⭐	The Hackney lifts its legs up high when it trots.

The Hackney is a mix of the Thoroughbred and the Norfolk Trotter. They were first bred in England to make elegant, lightweight horses. Hackneys have lots of spirit and good looks.

Haflinger

Haflingers get bored easily so they need lots of exercise!

Forever Fabulous Stats

Color	Shades of chestnut, from pale gold to liver	
Size	Up to 14 hands high	
♥♥♥	✓✓✓✓✓	
★★★	The Halfinger's mane is flaxen, which means it is a lighter color than its body.	

This charming breed comes from the mountains in Austria, Europe. Many villages in the mountains can only be reached by steep and narrow trails. Haflingers happily carry items along these trails. They are hard working and love people.

Hanoverian

This big, handsome horse was bred to pull carriages for a King!

Forever Fabulous Stats

Color	Brown, chestnut, bay, black, or gray
Size	Up to 17 hands high
❤️❤️	✓✓✓✓✓
⭐⭐	Hanoverians are calm and intelligent.

These beautiful horses are very graceful, so they were chosen to pull the royal carriages in Germany. Later, they pulled heavy weapons during World War I. Today they are wonderful sport horses, skilled at showjumping and dressage.

Highland Pony

Sturdy and strong, the Highland makes a great pony for the whole family.

Forever Fabulous Stats

Color	Dun, gray, black, brown, or bay
Size	Up to 14 hands high
♥♥	✓✓✓✓
★★	The Queen of England breeds Highland Ponies.

Horses have lived in Scotland for over 1,000 years. They used to work on farms in the highlands. The Scottish Highlands is a cold region with many mountains, so these ponies have thick hair to keep them warm.

Icelandic

In Iceland there is no word for "pony," so the native animal is called a horse.

Forever Fabulous Stats

Color	All colors
Size	Up to 13 hands high
🤍🤍🤍	✓✓✓✓
⭐⭐⭐	The Icelandic has a fast gait named the *skeið*, which means "flying pace."

52

People in Iceland were not allowed to bring horses in from the outside world, so the island's little horse has stayed pure. Icelandic horses have five gaits, or speeds, including the *tölt*; a fast walk that is perfect for traveling across Iceland's rocky land.

Irish Draught

Despite its name, the Irish Draught is much more than just a strong draft horse.

Forever Fabulous Stats

Color	All solid colors
Size	Up to 16 hands high
♥♥♥	✓✓✓✓✓
★★★	The Irish Draught makes an excellent sport horse.

Farmers in Ireland needed a horse that was strong enough to help with farm work, but also smart enough to go hunting. Irish Draughts are just that! As well as having good looks, they are calm, obedient, and do well at sporting events.

Lipizzaner

These gorgeous animals are famous as the "dancing white horses" of Vienna, in Europe.

Forever Fabulous Stats

Color	Gray
Size	Up to 16 hands high
♥♥♥	✓✓✓✓✓
★★★	There is always one dark brown or black Lipizzaner at the Spanish Riding School.

The world-famous Spanish Riding School in Vienna uses the Lipizzaner in its shows. The horses perform amazing "airs above the ground" jumps. All Lipizzaners can be traced back to just six stallions.

Lusitano

The Lusitano is an extremely comfortable horse to ride.

Forever Fabulous Stats

Color	Gray or bay
Size	Up to 15 hands high
🖤🖤	✓✓✓✓✓
⭐⭐⭐	Lusitanos have been in lots of movies because they are easy to train.

This is the horse that gave us the myth of the centaur—a creature that is half-human, half-horse— because of the close bond between these horses and their riders. The Lusitano comes from what is now Portugal, in Europe. Horses from this area were so fast that people said they must be "born from the wind."

Marwari

India's elegant breed has been around since the 1100s.

Forever Fabulous Stats

Color	All colors
Size	Up to 15 hands high
♥♥♥	✓✓✓✓✓
★★★	The Marwari has an amazing homing instinct. It can always find its way home.

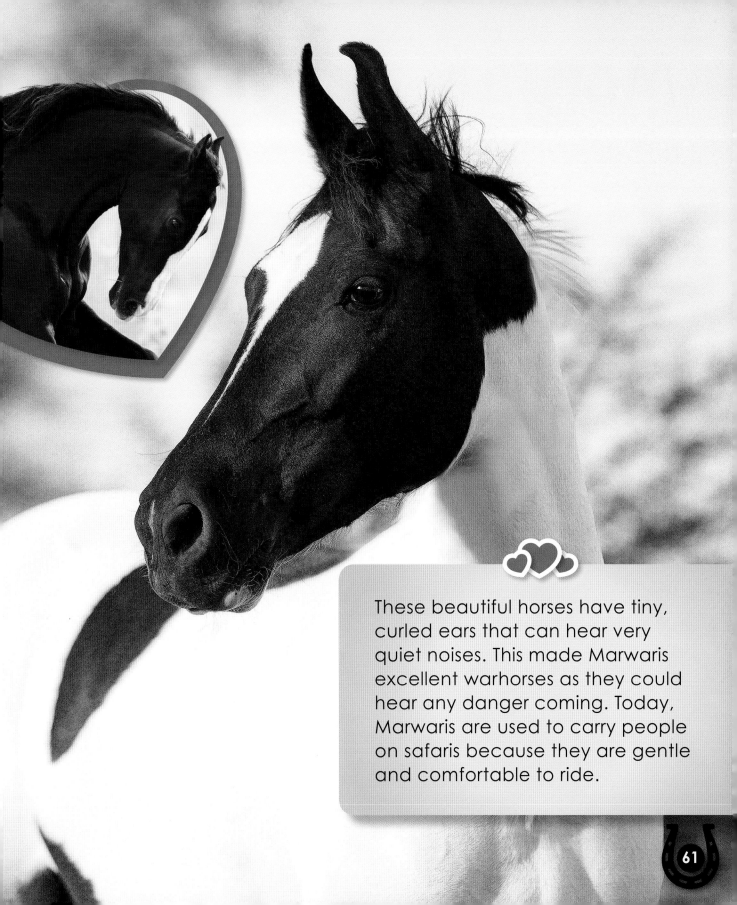

These beautiful horses have tiny, curled ears that can hear very quiet noises. This made Marwaris excellent warhorses as they could hear any danger coming. Today, Marwaris are used to carry people on safaris because they are gentle and comfortable to ride.

Morgan

This American breed has it all—speed, stamina, and good looks!

Forever Fabulous Stats

Color	All colors
Size	Up to 15 hands high
♥♥♥	✓✓✓✓
★★★	The first ever Morgan horse, named Figure, lived to the age of 32.

Horses were once known by their owner's name. The "Justin Morgan Horse," also named Figure, was famous in Vermont. He could outrun almost any other horse, even ones that were much bigger than him. Figure's children were very fast, too, so the Morgan horse became a popular breed.

Norwegian Fjord

These horses have striped markings on their legs and a black line down their backs.

Forever Fabulous Stats

Color	All shades of dun
Size	Up to 14 hands high
♥♥♥	✓✓✓✓
★★★	The Fjord's mane is unique; the middle hair is black and the outer hair is white.

Once used by the Vikings, this pretty horse is now a national symbol of Norway. They have neat heads, small ears, and beautiful eyes said to look like "mountain lakes on a midsummer evening, big and bright."

Orlov Trotter

This stunning breed was named after Count Orlov, who bred the horses in Russia.

Forever Fabulous Stats

Color	Mostly gray
Size	Up to 17 hands high
🤍☁️	✓✓✓✓✓
⭐⭐⭐	Orlov Trotters were prized for their fast but smooth trot.

Orlov Trotters were bred to be smart and speedy carriage horses. They were also used to pull sleds called troikas. These sleds were pulled by three horses, the middle one trotting and the horses on either side galloping.

Palomino

This glorious creature's coat shines like a new gold coin.

Forever Fabulous Stats

Color	All shades of gold, with white manes and tails
Size	All sizes
🖤🖤🖤	✓✓✓✓
⭐⭐⭐	The golden palomino color is also known as "isabella."

These golden horses have been popular for more than 600 years. Palominos were once so highly prized that only royalty was allowed to own them. The golden palomino color is found in most modern breeds, apart from the Thoroughbred and Arab.

Paso Fino

Paso Fino means "fine step," and this horse definitely has one!

Forever Fabulous Stats

Color	All colors
Size	Up to 15 hands high
♥♥♥	✓✓✓✓✓
★★★	The Paso Fino is known as the most comfortable riding horse in the world.

Like many American breeds, the wonderful Paso Fino was originally from Spain. Today's Paso is extremely handsome with a small head, long neck, sleek body, and strong legs. Paso Finos have more than four gaits which are all very comfortable for the rider.

Percheron

The Percheron is a heavy horse, but it has a very long neck and thin legs.

Forever Fabulous Stats

Color	Gray or black
Size	Up to 18 hands high
♥♥♥	✓✓✓✓✓
★★★	Percherons can live up to 30 years old!

The Percheron is the oldest draft breed in the world, and perhaps the most beautiful. These heavy horses were originally used to carry knights in armor into battle.

Peruvian Paso

Until around 40 years ago, this superb horse was unheard of outside Peru, in South America.

Forever Fabulous Stats

Color	All solid colors
Size	Up to 15 hands high
🖤🖤	✓✓✓✓✓
⭐⭐⭐	When the Inca tribe first saw horses, they were terrified of them!

Horses were first brought to Peru in 1531. Because of their stamina and speed, they were ridden around huge farms. The Paso is now the national horse of Peru. They have a gait known as the "termino," where the front legs move outward, like your arms when you swim.

Pony of the Americas

The first Pony of the Americas had a mark that looked like a handprint on his rump.

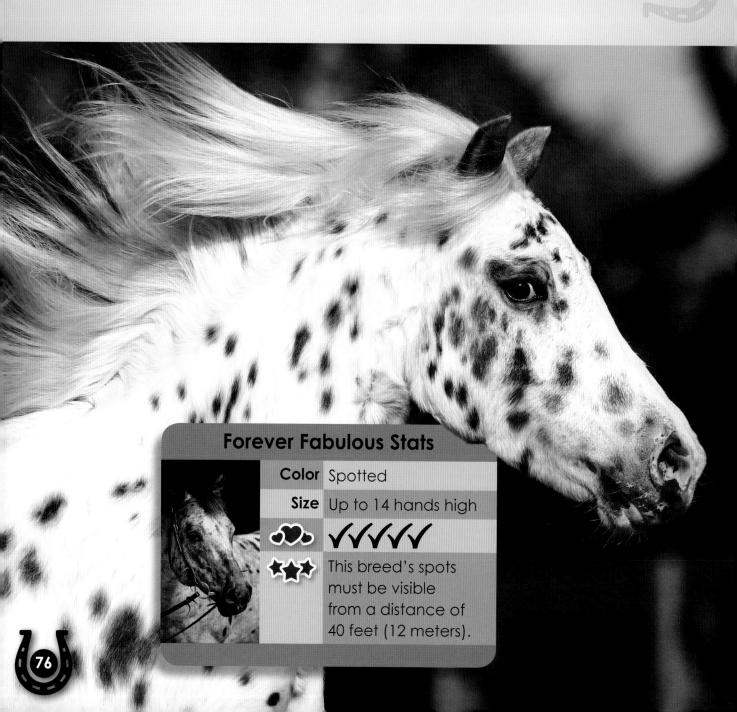

Forever Fabulous Stats

Color	Spotted
Size	Up to 14 hands high
🖤☁️	✓✓✓✓✓
⭐⭐	This breed's spots must be visible from a distance of 40 feet (12 meters).

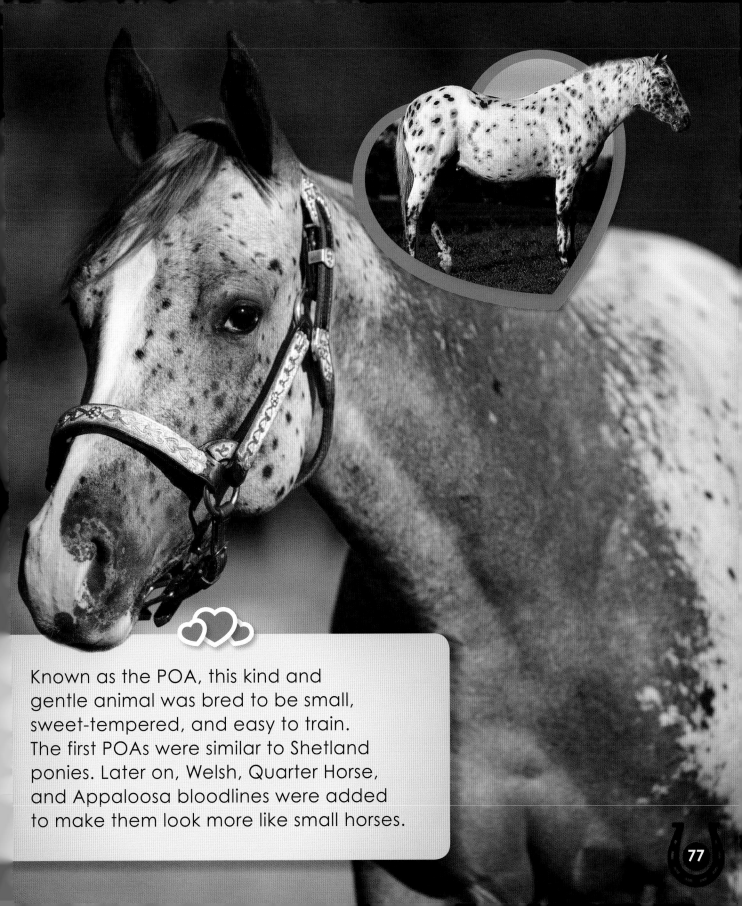

Known as the POA, this kind and
gentle animal was bred to be small,
sweet-tempered, and easy to train.
The first POAs were similar to Shetland
ponies. Later on, Welsh, Quarter Horse,
and Appaloosa bloodlines were added
to make them look more like small horses.

Przewalski's Horse

This is probably the last truly wild horse in the world.

Forever Fabulous Stats

Color	Dun, with black markings
Size	Up to 14 hands high
♥♥	✓✓✓✓✓
★★	There are fewer than 1,500 Przewalskis left in the world.

Przewalski's horses have a black line down their backs, known as a dorsal stripe. This breed was named for a Russian explorer who saw herds of strange-looking horses in China and Mongolia. They became extinct in the wild, but were reintroduced in the 1990s.

Rocky Mountain Horse

Good-looking, kind, and lovely to ride, the Rocky Mountain is the perfect trekking horse.

Forever Fabulous Stats

Color	All colors
Size	Up to 16 hands high
🐴🐴🐴	✓✓✓✓✓
⭐⭐⭐	Many of these horses are chocolate-brown with a golden mane and tail.

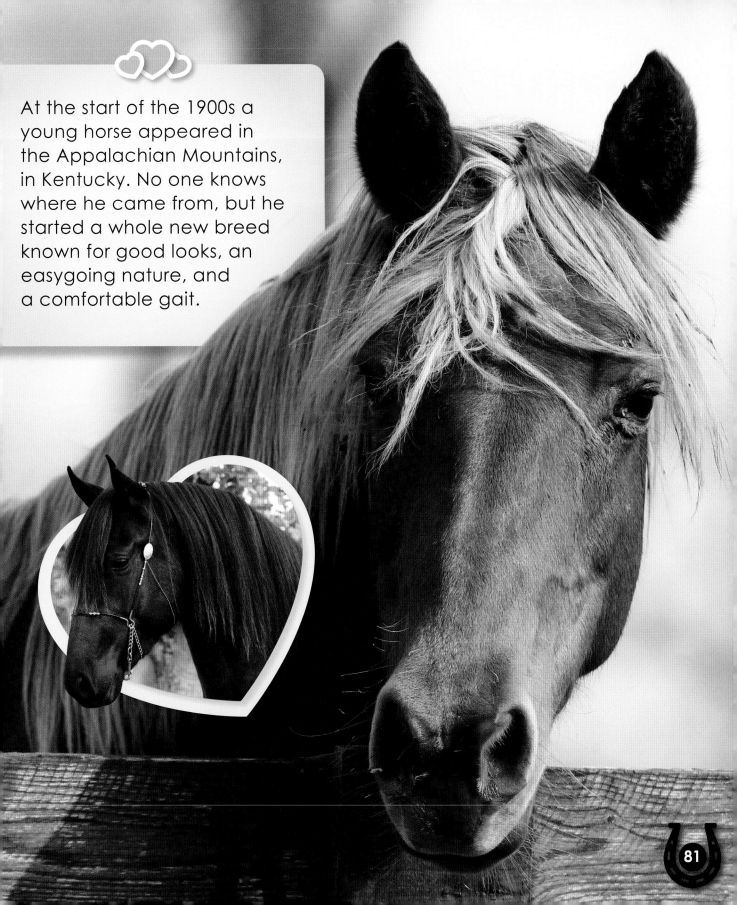

At the start of the 1900s a young horse appeared in the Appalachian Mountains, in Kentucky. No one knows where he came from, but he started a whole new breed known for good looks, an easygoing nature, and a comfortable gait.

Standardbred

Like the Thoroughbred, this neat little horse is built for speed.

Forever Fabulous Stats

Color	Bay, brown, or black
Size	Up to 15 hands high
♥♥♥	✓✓✓✓
★★★	Every Standardbred can be traced back to a horse named Hambleton 10.

In many North American cities there is a road named "Race Street." Owners used to race their horses down these streets to prove whose was the fastest. These horses were named Standardbred because they had to reach a standard time for the distance of one mile.

Shetland

The Shetland pony was so prized that you could be fined for cutting off its tail hair!

Forever Fabulous Stats

Color	All colors
Size	10 hands high
♥♥♥	✓✓✓✓
★★★	Their tail hairs were once used as fishing lines.

Shetland ponies have lived on the island of Shetland, off the coast of Scotland, for at least 2,000 years. They are hardy animals and can live on little food. They are also very strong for their size. Today there are standard Shetlands and miniature Shetlands. Miniature Shetlands are only 38 inches (96 centimeters) tall.

Shire

The biggest horse in the world was a Shire named Mammoth. He was 21.2 hands high!

Forever Fabulous Stats

Color	Bay, brown, black, or gray	
Size	18 hands high or more	
🖤🖤	✓✓✓✓✓	
⭐⭐⭐	Huge horses like the Shire were used to carry knights in heavy armor.	

The Shire is the largest breed from Great Britain. They were once called Great Horses, and later became known as the English Black. They were used to farm the land as they are stronger and more intelligent than oxen. Shires have hair, or "feathers", on their feet to protect them from the wet ground or from thorns and brambles.

Suffolk

All modern Suffolks can be traced back to one stallion, known as Crisp's Horse.

Forever Fabulous Stats

Color	All shades of chesnut
Size	Up to 16 hands high
🖤🖤	✓✓✓✓
⭐⭐⭐	The Suffolk is one of the oldest draft breeds in the world.

The Suffolk is a handsome, stocky little creature. Unlike other draft breeds, Suffolks have no long hair on their lower legs. All Suffolks are a glossy brown color, called chesnut. They were once called the Suffolk Sorrel.

Tennessee Walking Horse

The "Walker" was the first horse breed to be named after an American state.

Forever Fabulous Stats

Color	All colors
Size	Up to 17 hands high
♥♥♥	✓✓✓✓✓
★★★	Plantation owners would ride Tennessee Walkers around their land to check their crops.

People say, if you ride a Tennessee Walking Horse today, you'll buy one tomorrow, because it is so delightful to ride! It has three gaits, the flat-foot walk, the running walk, and the smooth canter. The flat-foot walk is very comfortable for the rider.

Thoroughbred

This wonderful horse can gallop at up to 40 miles per hour!

Forever Fabulous Stats

Color	All solid colors except palomino
Size	16 hands high
♥♥♥	✓✓✓✓✓
★★★	The first Thoroughbred was brought to North America in 1730.

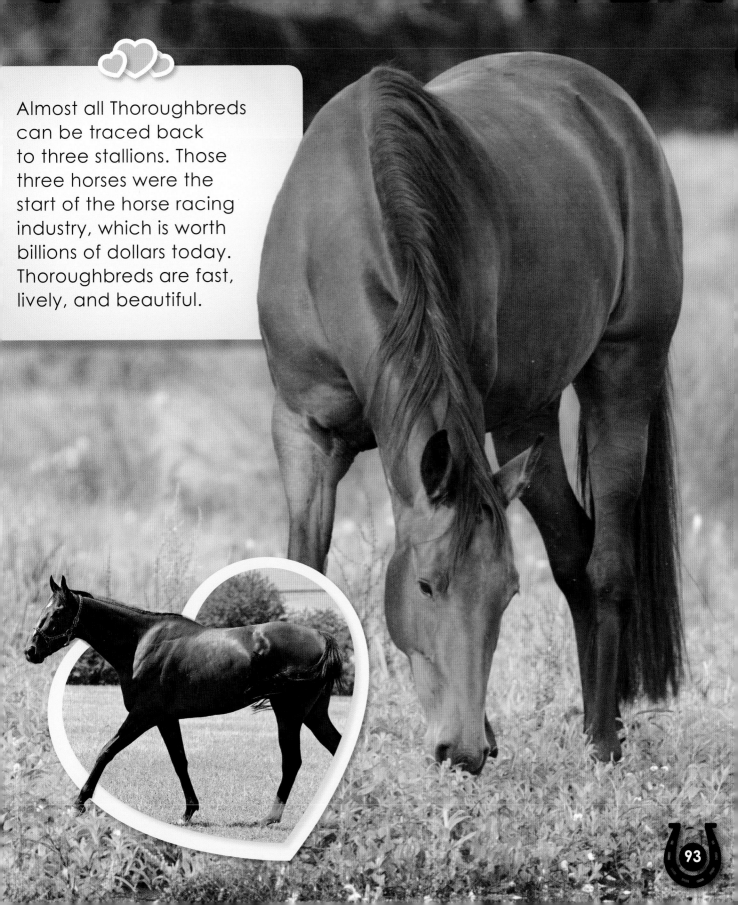

Almost all Thoroughbreds can be traced back to three stallions. Those three horses were the start of the horse racing industry, which is worth billions of dollars today. Thoroughbreds are fast, lively, and beautiful.

Welsh Mountain Pony

With its sweet nature, the Welsh Mountain is a perfect first pony to own.

Forever Fabulous Stats

Color	All solid colors
Size	12 hands high
🖤🖤	✓✓✓✓
⭐⭐	Despite being small, the Welsh Mountain can carry heavy weights.

Welsh Mountain Ponies are a pretty breed. They have a sweet nature with a mischievous side. They enjoy being with people and love to be made a fuss of. They are intelligent, too, and will look after their rider.

Picture Credits